ERROL HOWARD

PROGRAMMING WITH PYTHON

Master the Basics and Beyond with
Hands-On Projects and Expert Guidance
(2024 Guide for Beginners)

Copyright © 2024 by Errol Howard

All rights reserved. No part of this publication may be reproduced, stored or transmitted in any form or by any means, electronic, mechanical, photocopying, recording, scanning, or otherwise without written permission from the publisher. It is illegal to copy this book, post it to a website, or distribute it by any other means without permission.

First edition

This book was professionally typeset on Reedsy.
Find out more at reedsy.com

Contents

1 **Chapter 1** 1
   WHAT ARE SCRIPTING LANGUAGES? 1
   WHY CHOOSE PYTHON? 3
   EXAMPLE PROGRAM CODE 4
   PYTHON LISTS 5
   PYTHON BLOCKS 6
   PYTHON'S INTERACTIVE MODE 8
   USING PYTHON AS A CALCULATOR 11

2 **Chapter 2** 13
   EXAMPLE CODE 13
   COMMAND LINE ARGUMENTS 16
   INTODUCTION TO FILE MANIPULATION ... 16
   PYTHON 17
   INTERACTIVITY 18
   VARIABLES 18
   #Function 'type' 20
   # Help function 21
   ESTABLISHING A WORKING DIRECTORY ... 21
   Slicing 24
   # STRINGS 27
   # FUNCTION 'LIST' 30
   TUPLE 31
   # SETS 33
   # DICTIONARIES 34

#NUMBERS	36
# OPERATORS	38
# BITWISE OPERATORS	39
# ASSIGNMENT OPERATORS:	40
3 Chapter 3	42
CONDITIONAL INSTRUCTIONS AND LOOPS	42
# IF	43
#If... Else	44
#ELIF	44
# FOR	45
# ENUMERATE	48
# WHILE	49
# 'else' clause	51
4 Chapter 4	53
LIST COMPREHENSION	53
# IMPORT	54
EXCEPTIONS	57
EXCEPTION HANDLING	58
FUNCTIONS	61
Python Functions	61
# Built-in Functions Overview	65
Default Boolean functions:	65
SORTING FUNCTIONS:	67
# THE CLASSES	68
ADDING A METHOD TO THE CLASS	70
# CLASS METHODS	72
# PROPERTIES	75
# INPUT AND OUTPUT	78
# FILE	78
5 Chapter 5	81
FINDING ERRORS	81

Python's Native Debugger, PDB	82
Core Components	82
USING PDB MACROS	86
The type() function	88
Using PDB with Emacs	88

1

Chapter 1

WHAT ARE SCRIPTING LANGUAGES?

Scripting languages like C and C++ offer programmers the ability to write code with detailed precision, resulting in efficient execution speeds, especially with C. However, in numerous applications, execution speed isn't crucial, and many developers might prefer a higher-level approach. For instance, in text manipulation tasks, C/C++ focus on individual characters, whereas languages such as Perl and Python operate based on lines of text and words within those lines. While it's possible to handle lines and words in C/C++, it generally requires more effort compared to these other languages.

The term "scripting language" lacks a formal definition, but some common characteristics include:

- Predominantly used for tasks like systems administration, web development, and word processing.
- Relaxed variable typing, with minimal differentiation between integer, floating point, or string variables. Arrays can contain a mix of different data types, like integers and strings. Functions can yield nonscalar outputs, such as matrices, and nonscalar values can serve as loop indices, among other features.
- Incorporation of numerous high-level operations within the language, like string concatenation and stack push/pop.
- Typically interpreted rather than compiled to the host machine's instruction set.

CHAPTER 1

WHY CHOOSE PYTHON?

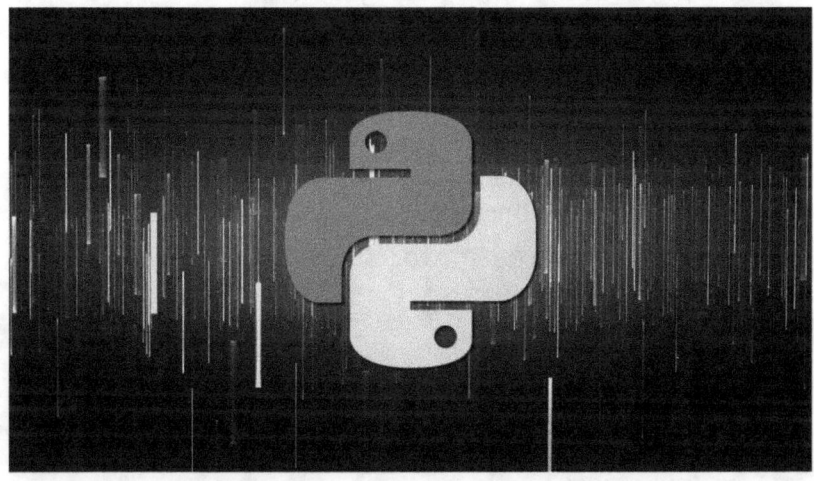

Perl was the initial scripting language that gained significant popularity. While it remains in use today, Python and Ruby have taken center stage as the current favored languages, with Ruby bearing similarities to Python. Many developers, myself included, find Python more appealing than Perl due to its cleaner and more refined nature. Python has garnered substantial adoption among Google's developer community.

Advocates of Python, often referred to as Python enthusiasts, assert that Python's clarity and the pleasure it brings while coding make it suitable for all programming tasks, not merely scripting. They argue its superiority over languages like C or C++. In my view, C++ seems fragmented with its components not fitting seamlessly, while Java, although more refined, is overly restrictive due to its strong typing, which can impede clear programming. I was encouraged to find Eric Raymond, a prominent figure in the open-source movement, sharing similar sentiments about C++, Java, and Python.

EXAMPLE PROGRAM CODE

Consider a simple demonstration. If you aim to determine values for x when it ranges from 0.0 to 0.9, you can achieve this using the subsequent code:

```
for i in range(10):
    x = 0.1 * i
    print(x)
    x / (1 - x * x)
```

Save this code in a file named, let's say, **demo.py**, and execute it by entering **python demo.py** in the command line interface. The output will appear as follows:

```
0.0
0.0
0.1
0.10101010101
0.2
0.208333333333
0.3
0.32967032967
0.4
0.47619047619
0.5
0.666666666667
```

```
0.6
0.9375
0.7
1.37254901961
0.8
2.22222222222
0.9
4.73684210526
```

PYTHON LISTS

How does this code operate? Python's **range()** function exemplifies Python3's approach to lists, which are essentially arrays but not labeled as such. Lists are integral to Python, so when you encounter the term "list," don't mistake it for the ordinary English word. Always perceive it as the Python-specific list construct.

The **range()** function from Python generates a list of consecutive integers. In this instance, it produces the list [0,1,2,3,4,5,6,7,8,9]. Note that this format signifies Python's standard notation for lists: a collection of items (which could vary from numbers to other entities), separated by commas and enclosed within parentheses. Therefore, the for-loop statement mentioned earlier is identical to:

```
for i in [0,1,2,3,4,5,6,7,8,9]:
```

This implies that the loop will iterate 10 times, with i initially set to 0 and progressing subsequently. If we had **for i in [2,3,6]:**, the loop would iterate three times, with i assuming the values 2, 3, and 6.

Python also incorporates a while loop structure, and similarly, it offers a break statement akin to that found in C/C++, which allows for an early exit from loops.

Example
```
x = 5
while 1:
x += 1
if x == 8:
print(x)
break
```

If one wishes to execute no operations at all, the pass keyword comes into play, exemplified by: class x(y): pass ensuring the class is not empty.

PYTHON BLOCKS

Shift your focus to the seemingly harmless colon found at the end of the 'for' line, marking the start of a block. In contrast to languages such as C/C++ and Perl that employ curly braces for block definition, Python utilizes a colon followed by indentation. This colon serves as a signal to the Python interpreter, informing it that a block starts in the subsequent line. I've indented that line and the subsequent two lines to its right, indicating that these three lines constitute a block.

I've opted for a three-space indentation, but the specific number isn't crucial as long as consistency is maintained. For instance, had I written:

```
for i in range(10):print 0.1*i
   print g(0.1*i)
```

The Python interpreter would flag it as a syntax error due to inconsistent indentation. If there's a sub-block within a block, I can indent slightly more to the right. For example:

```
for i in range(10):
    if i%2 == 1:
        print 0.1*i
        print g(0.1*i)
```

In this scenario, I'm only displaying cases where 'i' is an odd number; '%' functions as the modulo operator similar to C/C++. Once again, observe the colon at the 'if' line's end and the increased indentation of the two print statements compared to the 'if' line.

Additionally, unlike in C/C++ and Perl, Python doesn't use semicolons to terminate instructions. A new line denotes a fresh instruction. Should you require an extended line, utilize the backslash character for continuation, like so:

```
x = y + \
z
```

PYTHON'S INTERACTIVE MODE

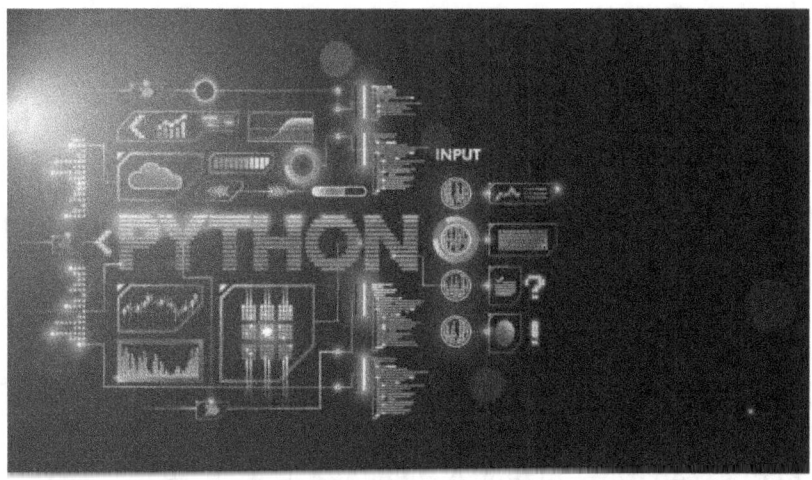

Python also provides an interactive mode, which is a standout feature. While it's not typically the primary way to use Python, it serves as a valuable tool for quick experimentation with functionalities to understand them better. Whenever you're uncertain about the behavior of something, the mantra should be, "When in doubt, try it!" Interactive mode facilitates this experimentation efficiently.

In this guide, we'll frequently utilize interactive mode to easily demonstrate specific features. Rather than executing a program from the command line in batch mode, as previously shown, you can input and execute code directly in interactive mode.

For instance:

```
% python
>>> for i in range(10):
...     x = 0.1*i
...     print(x)
...     print(x/(1-x*x))
...
0.0
0.0
0.1
0.10101010101
0.2
0.208333333333
0.3
0.32967032967
0.4
0.47619047619
0.5
0.666666666667
0.6
0.9375
0.7
1.37254901961
0.8
2.22222222222
0.9
4.73684210526
>>>
```

In this example, I initiated Python, which displayed its interactive prompt »>. Then, I simply entered the code line by line. Each time I was inside a code block, it presented a specific "..." prompt. When I entered a blank line after my code, Python recognized that I had finished and executed the code.

In interactive mode, you can navigate through the command

history using the cursor keys, which helps reduce keystrokes. To exit interactive Python, you can press **ctrl+d**.

Moreover, in interactive mode, simply referencing or generating an object or even an expression without assigning it will result in its value being displayed without needing a print statement.
   For example:

```
>>> for i in range(4):
...     3*i
...
0
3
6
9
```

This behavior isn't limited to expressions; it applies to generic objects as well.
   For instance:

```kotlin
>> open('x')
<open file 'x', mode 'r' at 0xb7eaf3c8>.
```

Here, we opened the file 'x', creating an object file. Since we didn't assign the object to a variable like **f**, as commonly done with **f = open('x')**, the object's details were displayed. Alternatively, we could have achieved the same result with:

```
>>> f = open('x')
>>> f
```

```
<open file 'x', mode 'r' at 0xb7f2a3c8>.
```

USING PYTHON AS A CALCULATOR

One of the advantages of Python is its ability to function as an efficient calculator, a feature I frequently utilize. For instance, to determine 5% of $88.88, one can input:

```
>>> 1.05*88.88
93.323999999999998
```

Additionally, Python facilitates swift conversions between decimals and hexadecimals.

```
>>> 0x12
18
>>> hex(18)
'0x12'
```

When it comes to mathematical operations beyond basic calculations, it's necessary to "import" the Python math library initially. This procedure is comparable to what's done in C/C++, where a library inclusion is mandated in the source code via an #include directive and subsequently linked in the machine code. After importing the math library, functions like sqrt() and sin() must be referenced with the prefix "math."

```
>> import math
>>> math.sqrt(88)
9.3808315196468595
>>> math.sin(2.5)
```

0.59847214410395655

2

Chapter 2

EXAMPLE CODE

The following script demonstrates an example program. Its purpose is to read a specified text file from the command line and then display the count of both lines and words within the file:

```
1 # reads in the text file whose name was specified in the command line,
2 # and reports the number of lines and words.
3
4 import sys
5
6 def checkline():
7     global line_count
8     global word_count
9     words = line.split()
10     word_count += len(words)
11
12 line_count = 0
13 word_count = 0
14
15 file = open(sys.argv[1])
16 file_lines = file.readlines()
17 line_count = len(file_lines)
18
for line in file_lines:
    checkline()

print(line_count, word_count)
```

For instance, assuming the script is saved as "example.py" and we have a text file named "text_file.txt" containing the text:

```
This is a
sample text
file
```

When executing the script with this file, the output would be:

```
python example.py text_file.txt
```

At first glance, the code resembles that of a C/C++ program: it begins with an import statement, similar to the #include directive in C/C++, which establishes a link during compilation. Following this is the definition of a function and then the primary program labeled "main." While this perspective is accurate, it's essential to understand that the Python interpreter processes commands sequentially, starting from the top. For instance, executing an import statement could involve running some code if the imported module contains executable code. While defining a function with the "def" statement doesn't immediately run any code, the act of creating the function is still considered an execution.

This program showcases several features not present in the initial example:

- Utilization of command-line arguments
- Mechanisms for file manipulation
- Further exploration of lists
- Function definition
- Incorporation of libraries
- Introduction to program purpose

I'll delve into these aspects in upcoming sections.

COMMAND LINE ARGUMENTS

Firstly, let's clarify what sys.argv is. Python offers a module, or library, named sys, which includes a variable named argv. This variable is a Python list, resembling argv in C/C++, where the first element (index 0) is the script's name, like "tme.py", and so forth, much like in C/C++. In our example, if we initiate our program with file "x", sys.argv[1] would contain the string 'x'. It's worth noting that in Python, strings are typically enclosed within quotation marks. Since sys is not loaded automatically, we require the import statement.

Both in C/C++ and Python, command-line arguments are strings by default. If these strings were meant to represent numerical values, conversion would be necessary. For instance, if we had an integer argument in C/C++, we'd use atoi(); in Python, we'd utilize int(). For floating-point numbers in Python, the appropriate conversion function would be float().

INTODUCTION TO FILE MANIPULATION

The open() function resembles its counterpart in C/C++. When we execute the line f = open(sys.argv[1]), we instantiate a file object and assign it to the variable f. Utilizing the readlines() method of the file class results in a list containing the lines from the file. It's important to note that "list" is a recognized term in Python. Each line in the file is a string, and these strings constitute the elements of the list. Given that the file comprises five lines, invoking readlines() returns a list with five elements: ['', 'This is an', 'example of', 'text file', ''] (Each string includes an end-of-line character [EOL], although it's not visible here).

___ _

CHAPTER 2

```
# /__|___ ___||__ ___
# | (_/ -_) -_) / /(_-<
# _____|_\_\/__/
# /_\ __ ___ __||___ _ __ __
# / _ \/ _| _' / _' / -_)' \ | | |
# /_/\_\__\__,_\__,_\___|_|_|_\_,|
# |__/
# +———————————-+
| PYTHON LANGUAGE
# +———————————-+
```

PYTHON

Python is a programming language known for its interpretive nature, interactivity, and object-oriented design.

It boasts features such as modules, exceptions, dynamic typing, high-level data types, classes, and a straightforward syntax.

Furthermore, Python offers extensibility through integration with languages like C, C++, and Java, making it suitable for a variety of applications, including configuration tasks. Additionally, Python is adaptable and can be embedded into various environments.

INTERACTIVITY

Interactivity involves performing mathematical operations and executing code snippets.
   result1 = 14 + 10
   result2 = 9 * 9

Hello World
   print("Hello World!")

Python code computes the sum of 14 and 10, storing the result in the variable **result1**, and calculates the product of 9 and 9, storing the result in the variable **result2**.
   Following that, in the "Hello World" section, the code prints the message "Hello World!" to the console, demonstrating a simple output statement in Python.

VARIABLES

```
message = "Hello World!"
print(message)

number = 281
print(number)

decimal_number = 21.78
print(decimal_number)
```

Notes on Variables

- Variable names begin with letters or underscores and are case-sensitive.
- Automatic type casting occurs in Python!

```
a = 22
b = 23.22
result = a + b
print(result)
```

Comments

In Python, anything written after a # symbol is considered a comment and will not be executed.

More about Variables

```
city = "Como"
print(city)

city = "Rome"
print(city)
```

```
print(number + decimal_number)
print(10 + decimal_number)

name = "Aldo"
last_name = "Serra"
print(name + last_name)
print(name + " " + last_name)
```

Deleting a Variable

If you attempt to print a deleted variable, Python will raise an error.

```
city = "Milan"
print(city)

del city
# This will raise an error since 'city' is deleted.
# print(city)
```

#Function 'type'

The 'type' function showcases the data type of the provided object.

```
type(5)
type("hello")
type(number)
type(decimal_number)
type(message)
type(name)
type = 5   # <--- Is this intended?
# Resolves to 'del type'
```

- when using 'type(5)', it will display that 5 is an integer.
- 'type("hello")' reveals that "hello" is a string.

The 'type' function can be applied to various objects like numbers, decimal numbers, messages, and names to determine their respective data types.

However, it's essential not to overwrite built-in functions, like mistakenly assigning 'type' to the value 5, which could lead to issues.

Help function

The 'help' function provides a detailed description and functionality of the specified object.

```
# Displays the description and functionality of the
object passed as a parameter.
help(print)   # (Press 'q' to exit help in the
terminal)
```

Exploring new features

```
import math
math.sqrt(100)
math.pow(5, 3)
```

ESTABLISHING A WORKING DIRECTORY

```python
import os
os.getcwd()
os.chdir("a/")
os.getcwd()
```

Checking Python Version

```python
import sys
print(sys.version)
```

Lists in Python

```python
# A sequential collection of diverse items
list_items = [15, 7, 19, 75]
print(list_items)

various = [19, "hello", list_items]
print(various)
```

Adding Elements to Lists

```python
various.append(124.75)
print(various)

import math
various.append(math)
print(various)
```

Understanding Object Attributes in Python

```python
# The dot, '.', distinguishes between an object and
its property or method
```

Accessing List Elements

```
list_items[0]
list_items[1]
various[1]
list_items[-1]
```

Using the 'len' Function

```
# Determines the length of a list
len(list_items)
len(various)
```

Using the ':' Symbol for Slicing

```
list_items[0:2]
list_items[1:3]
list_items[1:]
list_items[:2]
list_items[:]
```

Copying Lists

```
# The last method can be employed to replicate a list:
list_copy = list_items[:]
```

Slicing

It allows you to manipulate lists effectively in Python. Consider a list containing elements:

```
list_example = ["P", "Y", "T", "H", "O", "N", "!"]
'''
 0   1   2   3   4   5   6
 |   |   |   |   |   |   |
 | P | Y | T | H | O | N | !|
 |   |   |   |   |   |   |
-7  -6  -5  -4  -3  -2  -1
'''
```

Assign elements

```
list_copy = list_example[:]
list_copy[0:2] = [13, "abc"]
```

Insert elements

```
list_copy[1:1] = [1, 2, 3]   # Insert at index 1
# Delete elements
list_copy[1:3] = []  # Delete elements at index 1 and 2
# E.g., delete the last two elements
list_copy[-2:] = []
```

Insert method

```
list_example.insert(3, "new")
list_example.insert(42, "bottom")   # Caution: Out-of-range index
```

Method 'extend' adds element(s) to the list

```
addition = ["x", "y", "z"]
list_example.extend(addition)
```

Method 'remove' removes the desired element

```
list_example.remove("new")
```

Pop method: Extracts the last element (and removes it from the list)

```
list_example.pop()
```

Method 'count' counts how many times the desired item appears in the list

```
list_example.count(7)
```

Method 'index' returns the index of the desired element

```
list_example.index("hello")   # Raises ValueError if not found
```

Reverse method

```
list_example.reverse()
```

Sort method

```
numbers = [1, 7, 54, 3, 21, 500, 12, 4, 8]
numbers.sort()
list_example.sort()
```

Note: Sort does not work in heterogeneous lists

```
numbers.append("s")
# numbers.sort()   # Raises TypeError due to mixed data types
```

Operator 'in'

```
21 in numbers    # Returns True
987 in numbers   # Returns False
```

Empty list

```
empty_list = []
# Or
```

```
empty_list = list()
```

STRINGS

The following code illustrates various operations on strings:

```
# Defining a string
string = "0123456789"

# Extracting the first 5 characters
string[:5]

# Extracting the last 5 characters
string[-5:]

# Extracting all characters except the first and last
one
string[1:-1]

# Slicing with three parameters: start, stop, and step
string[0:8:2]
string[::2]   # Every 2 characters
string[1::2]  # Every 2 characters starting from the
second one
```

Immutable nature of strings

```
# Attempting to change a character at a specific index
# Results in an error, so we edit the string instead
string[2] = "c"
string_edited = string[:2] + "c" + string[3:]
```

Defining strings with various quotes

```python
string1 = "Pizza with fries"
string2 = 'Special Pizza'
string3 = "Pizzas:\n - white\n - red"
```

Printing a multiline string

```python
print(string3)
```

Example of a multiline string with triple quotes

```python
string4 = """
Write strings
across multiple lines
with superscripts: 'pizza
and double quotes: "calzone"!
"""
```

String repetition

```python
string6 = "pizza"
string6 * 5

# Finding a substring within a string
string1.find("p")
```

Methods for changing case

```python
string1.lower()
string1.upper()
string1.title()
string1.capitalize()
string1.swapcase()
```

Stripping spaces from a string

```
string7 = " kebab "
string7.strip()
```

Replacing substrings within a string

```
string1.replace("chips", "mushrooms")
```

Splitting and joining strings

```
string1.split(" ")
string1.split("a")
```

Example: extracting components from an email address

```
string8 = "abc@ccc.ddd.com"
email_components = string8.split("@")
print(email_components)
provider = email_components[1].split(".")
print(provider[-1])
```

Modifying an email address

```
email_address = "mario.geeks@google.com"
components_mail = email_address.split("@")
user_data = components_mail[0]
data_provider = components_mail[1]
print(user_data, data_provider)
last_name = user_data.split(".")[1]
provider = data_provider.split(".")[0]
domain = data_provider.split(".")[1]
```

Demonstrating immutability by replacing a portion of the email address

```
email_address.replace(".com", ".it")
print(email_address)
new_mail_address = email_address.replace(".com", ".it")
print(new_mail_address)
```

Modifying an email address by replacing the provider

```
geeks_mail = email_address.replace(provider, "geeksmail")
print(geeks_mail)
```

#Joining strings with a specified separator

```
divisor = "/"
data_num = ["27", "10", "1977"]
divider.join(data_num)
"-".join(data_num)
string6.join(data_num)
```

This code snippet covers various string operations and demonstrates the immutability of strings in Python.

FUNCTION 'LIST'

```
list("abcd")
list("PYTHON!")
```

Operator 'in'

```
"z" in string6
```

Using list methods on the string

```
", ".join(data_num)
"Pizza and kebab".split(" ")
```

'Format' method

```
user1 = "Sabrina"
"User {} has just logged in.".format(user1)

user2 = "Michele"
"User {} has just logged in.".format(user2)
```

If we want to use more than one:

```
"Users {0} and {1} have just
connected.".format(user1, user2)
"Users {0} and {1} have just logged in. User {0} has
administrator privileges.".format(user1, user2)
```

TUPLE

- Tuples are ordered sequences of heterogeneous objects, similar to lists but immutable, unlike lists and similar to strings.
- They serve as a data type intermediate between strings and lists.

Example:

```
tuple_example = (1, 2, 3, 4, 5)
```

Slicing

```
tuple_example[:3]   # Returns (1, 2, 3)
tuple_example[-1]   # Returns 5
```

Immutability

```
# Trying to modify a tuple will raise an error
# tuple_example[2] = "abc"   # This will raise an error
```

Count method

```
fibonacci = (1, 1, 2, 3, 5, 8, 13, 21)
fibonacci.count(8)     # Returns 1
fibonacci.count(1)     # Returns 2
fibonacci.count(100)   # Returns 0
```

Index method

```
fibonacci.index(13)   # Returns 6
```

Operator 'in'

```
5 in fibonacci   # Returns True
9 in fibonacci   # Returns False
```

Tuple with only one element

```
single = (1,)   # Note the comma after the element to
indicate it's a tuple with one element
```

SETS

Sets are a data type for managing groups of unordered elements without duplicates.

```
my_set = {"pizza", "kebab", "hamburger", "kebab"}
print(my_set)
```

Accessing elements in a set

```
# my_set[0] # This will raise an error as sets do not
support indexing
```

Creating a set from a string

```
letters = set("hello")
```

Union operator

```
small = {"mouse", "lizard"}
large = {"elephant", "whale"}
print(large | small)
```

Union with another set

```python
white = {"ermine", "mouse"}
print(small | white)
```

Difference operator

```python
print(small - white)
```

Intersection operator

```python
print(small & white)
```

Symmetrical difference operator (xor)

```python
print(small ^ white)
```

DICTIONARIES

Dictionaries serve as associative arrays, comprising objects paired with specific keys.

```python
contacts = {}   # or contacts = dict()
contacts["Sergio"] = "333-111222333"
contacts["Simona"] = "345-999944444"
print(contacts)

contacts["Sergio"]
contacts["David"] = "321-000222444"
```

Retrieve keys from a dictionary using the 'keys' method

```
contacts.keys()
```

Check for key existence using the 'in' operator

```
"Ada" in contacts
"Sergio" in contacts
```

Remove an entry from the dictionary

```
del contacts["Sergio"]

# Dictionaries can store any Python object, including
functions and classes.
# Keys must be immutable types like strings,
integers, or tuples.
```

The 'get' method retrieves a default value if the key is absent

```
inventory = {"t-shirt": 10,
             "coats": 8,
             "scarves": 7}

inventory["scarves"]
inventory["socks"]
inventory.get("socks", 0)
inventory.get("scarves", 0)
```

The 'set default' method retrieves and optionally adds a default value

```
inventory.setdefault("socks", 0)
inventory.setdefault("scarves", 0)
```

Retrieve values using the 'values' method

```
inventory.values()
sum(inventory.values())
```

The 'items' method returns key-value pairs as tuples

```
inventory.items()
```

Update dictionary entries using the 'update' method

```
inventory.update({"t-shirt": 4, "socks": 9})
```

#NUMBERS

```
# NUMBERS
2 ** 10
```

Integers have no size limit, constrained only by the computer's memory.

```
2 ** 10000
32.7854 / 9.738
```

Different numeral systems: hexadecimal, octal, and binary

```
0xff
0o77
```

```
0b110
```

Complex numbers

```
comp_num = 2.4 - 6.7j
comp_num.real
comp_num.imag
```

Exponential notation

```
3e2
7e10
```

Logical values

```
True
False
```

Absence of a value

```
None
var_value = None
```

Type conversions

```
a_tuple = ("x", "y", "z")
one_list = [18, 19, 20]
a_string = "1997"
a_whole = 42
un_decimal = 3.1416
```

```
tuple(one_list)
list(a_tuple)
int(a_string)
str(a_whole)
float(a_whole)
int(un_decimal)    # truncation
```

Multi-line comments: ''' comment '''

```
'''
This serves as a multi-line comment.
No need for the hash mark at the start of each line.
'''
```


OPERATORS

```
'''
Addition: +
Subtraction: -
Division: /
Multiplication: *
Modulo: %
Exponentiation: **
Floor Division: //
'''
```

Examples:

```
10 / 6        # Division
10 // 6       # Floor Division
7 % 3         # Modulo
```

COMPARISON OPERATORS

```
'''
<
>
==
>=
<=
!=
is
is not
in
not in
'''
```

Examples:

```
5 < 7
8 == 9
"hello" == "hello"
200 <= 200
"c" in "hello"
"c" not in "hello"
var = None
var is None
```

BITWISE OPERATORS

```
'''
and
or
xor
```

```
not
'''

5 < 2 and 10 >= 7
5 > 2 and 10 >= 7

age = 20
age > 17 and age < 19

eta = 18
eta >= 17 and eta <= 19
17 < age < 19

eta >= 17 or eta <= 19
5 < 2 or 10 >= 7

not 21 == 21
not eta == 18

age = 90
not (eta >= 17 and eta <= 19)

age = 18
not eta >= 17 and eta <= 19
```

ASSIGNMENT OPERATORS:

```
'''
=
+=
-=
/=
*=
```

CHAPTER 2

```
%=
**=
//=
'''

num = 5
num = num + 1
num += 1
num *= 10

price = 100
new_price = price * 0.8
price *= 0.8
price == new_price

num **= 2
```

3

Chapter 3

CONDITIONAL INSTRUCTIONS AND LOOPS

- **if**
- **elif**
- **else**
- **for**
- **while**
- **continue** and **break**

IF

CHAPTER 3

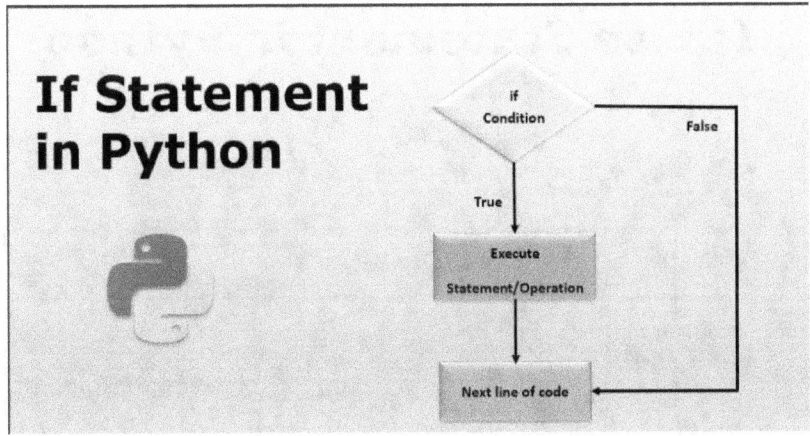

```
if condition:
    run action(s)

x = 5
y = 7
if x < y:
    print("x is less than y")

age = 17
if 17 <= age <= 19:
    print("eligible for tournament")
```

Note: Beware of indentation! If we get it wrong, the code won't work.

#If... Else

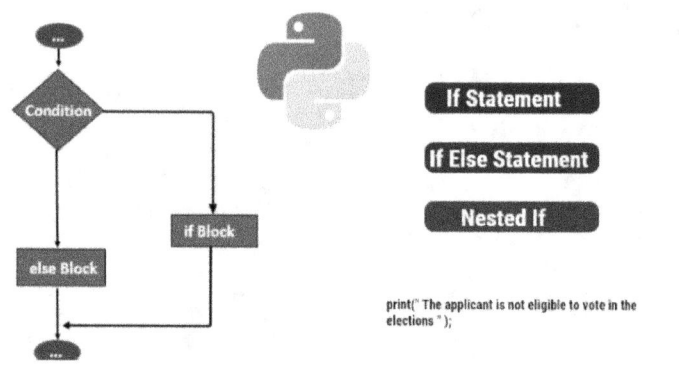

```
if condition:
    run action
else:
    perform other action

x = 5
y = 7
if x < y:
    print("x is less than y")
else:
    print("x is greater than or equal to y")
```

#ELIF

```
age = 16
if 17 <= age <= 19:
    print("eligible for tournament")
else:
    print("ineligible")
```

```
if condition:
    run action
elif other condition:
    perform other action
else:
    perform yet another action

temperature = 27
if temperature < 20:
    print("cold")
elif temperature > 30:
    print("hot")
else:
    print("optimal")

temperature = 27
if temperature < 20:
    print("cold")
elif temperature > 30:
    print("hot")
elif 20 < temperature < 30:
    print("optimal")
```

FOR

Perform one or more operations for a given number of times:

```
for element in iterable:
    perform action(s) on item
pythonCopy code
set_numbers = (1, 4, 6, 7, 2, 8)
for number in set_numbers:
    print(number)
```

```python
word = "Python"
for letter in word:
    print(letter + "!")

for number in range(4):
    print(number)

list(range(4))
list(range(3, 10))
list(range(2, 10, 2))
list(range(5, 0, -1))

address_book = {"John": "Doe", "Jane": "Doe"}
for key, value in address_book.items():
    print(key, value)

set_numbers = (1, 4, 6, 7, 2, 8)
for number in set_numbers:
    print("Original number:", number)
    double = number * 2
    print("Number doubled:", double)
print("I'm done.")

set_numbers = (1, 4, 6, 7, 2, 8)
for number in set_numbers:
    double = number * 2
    print("The double of {0} is equal to
    {1}.\n".format(number, double))
print("I'm done.")

prices = (20, 40, 50, 60, 190, 30)
discounted_prices = []
for price in prices:
    print("Original price: {}".format(price))
    discounted_prices.append(price * 0.8)
    print("Discounted price: {}".format(price * 0.8))
```

```
print("\nFinished.")

prices = (20, 40, 50, 60, 190, 30)
discounted_prices = []
discount = 0.9
for price in prices:
    print("Original price: {}".format(price))
    discounted_prices.append(price * discount)
    print("Discounted price:
    {}".format(discounted_prices[-1]))
print("\nFinished.")

prices = (20, 40, 50, 60, 190, 30)
discounted_prices = []
discount = 0.8  # this is actually the portion to be
paid
discount_print = round((1 - discount) * 100)
for price in prices:
    print("Original price: {}".format(price))
    discounted_prices.append(price * discount)
    print("Discounted price ({}%):
    {}".format(discount_print, discounted_prices[-1]))
print("\nFinished.")

prices = (20, 40, 50, 60, 190, 30)
discount1 = 37   # %
discount2 = 10
discounted_prices = []
for price in prices:
    print("Original price: {}".format(price))
    if price > 55:
        print("I am using a discount of
        {}%".format(discount2))
        discounted_prices.append(price * (100 -
        discount2) / 100)
    else:
        print("I am using a discount of
```

```
        {}%".format(discount1))
        discounted_prices.append(price * (100 -
        discount1) / 100)
    print("Discounted price:
    {}".format(discounted_prices[-1]))
print("\nFinished.")
```

ENUMERATE

To count the elements of a sequence while iterating

```
books = ["encyclopedia", "atlas", "dictionary"]
for book in books:
    print(book)
for counter, book in enumerate(books):
    print(counter, book)
```

Function 'zipper'

```
# To iterate over more than one list
pupils = ["Lucio", "Silvio", "Michela", "Natalia"]
courses = ["engineering", "medicine", "cinema", "law"]
years = [19, 22, 25, 21]
for pupil, course, age in zip(pupils, courses, years):
    print(pupil, "attends", course, "and is", age,
    "years old.")
```

Various ways to print specific line numbers

```
for num in range(10000):
    if num in [1000, 2000, 3000, 4000, 5000]:
        print("You are at line no.", num)
```

```
for num in range(10000):
    if num in list(range(1000, 10000, 1000)):
        print("You are at line no.", num)

for num in range(10000):
    if num % 1000 == 0:
        print("You are at line no.", num)
```

WHILE

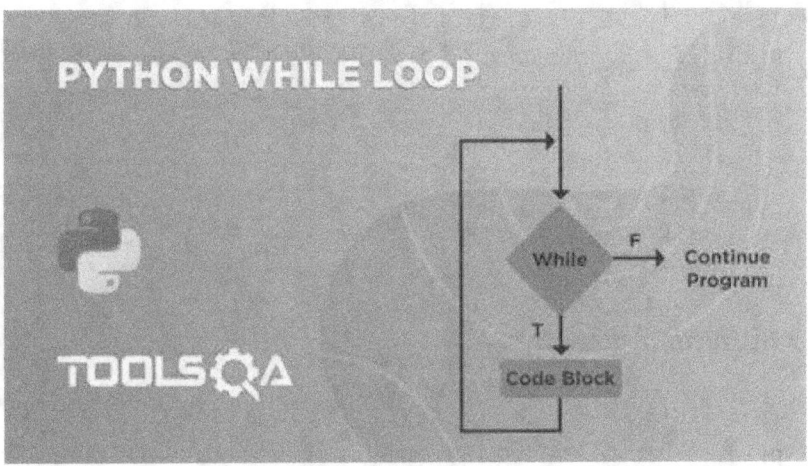

```
# Executes one or more operations until a condition
is met
'''
while condition == True:
    run action
'''
x = 1
```

```python
while x < 5:
    print(x)
    x += 1

# Checking for potential infinite loop
x = 7
while x > 5:
    print(x)
    x = x + 1
    if x == 10:   # Added a condition to exit the loop
        break
```

Instruction 'continue'

```python
list1 = [4, 5, 7, 8, 12, "abc", 15, 21, 45]
print("I will now print only the numbers:")
for item in list1:
    if item == "abc":
        continue
    else:
        print("-", item)
```

Instruction 'break'

```python
list1 = [4, 5, 7, 8, 12, "abc", 15, 21, 45]
print("This list contains only numbers:")
for item in list1:
    if item == "abc":
        print("Error! There are no numbers only!")
        break
    else:
        print("-", item)
```

'else' clause

```
# In a 'for' loop, it is executed at the end of the
loop
'''
for element in list:
    if element_has_a_certain_characteristic:
        print("found!")
        break
else:
    print("I looked everywhere, but it wasn't there")
'''
numbers_list = [1, 5, 7, 8, 10, 9, 14]
print("I'm looking for a number divisible by 3...")
for number in numbers_list:
    print("Checking the", number)
    if number % 3 == 0:
        print("Found:", number)
        break
else:
    print("There are no numbers divisible by 3")
```

Instruction 'pass'

```
# Used when we don't want a construct to do anything
x = 10
if x < 1:
    print("good")
if x == 10:
    # To be completed
    pass
```

Exercise

```
'''
Given an integer n, write a program that generates a
dictionary containing
keys from 1 to n (inclusive) and their corresponding
values as i*i.
Eventually, the program must print the dictionary.
Suppose the input given to the program is:
n = 7
'''

n = 7
result_dict = {i: i*i for i in range(1, n+1)}
print(result_dict)
```

4

Chapter 4

LIST COMPREHENSION

It's a syntactic construct that allows new lists to be constructed from other pre-existing lists.

```python
numbers = [1, 3, 4, 8, 9, 10, 16, 20, 31]
doubles = [num * 2 for num in numbers]
print(doubles)

even = [num for num in numbers if num % 2 == 0]
print(even)

discounted_prices = [num * 0.8 for num in numbers]
print(discounted_prices)
```

Set comprehension

```python
'''
Similar to list comprehension, but the final result
has no duplicates.
'''
rests = {num % 8 for num in numbers}
print(rests)
```

Dictionary comprehension

```python
prices = {"eggs": 12, "broccoli": 8, "apples": 5}
new_prices = {item: prices[item] * 2 for item in
prices.keys()}
new_prices = {item: price * 2 for item, price in
prices.items()}
```

IMPORT

It is used to import libraries that contain additional functions that can be useful to us.

```
import math

math.sqrt(144)
math.degrees(math.pi / 2)

from math import factorial

factorial(12)

from math import sqrt, degrees, pi

sqrt(144)
degrees(pi / 2)

import math as mt
from math import factorial as fct

fct(12)
```

Numpy

```
import numpy as np

my_list = [1, 2, 3]
array = np.array(my_list)
type(array)

np.arange(0, 11, 2)
np.zeros(5)
np.zeros((3, 4))
np.ones((3, 4))
np.linspace(0, 11, 10)
np.linspace(0, 11, 11)
np.linspace(0, 11, 100)
```

Random

```
np.random.randint(0, 10)   # minimum included, maximum excluded
np.random.randint(0, 1000)
np.random.randint(0, 1000, (3, 4))

np.random.seed(42)
np.random.randint(0, 100, 10)

np.random.seed(42)
array = np.random.randint(0, 100, 10)
array.max()
array.mean()
array.argmax()
array.reshape(2, 5)

mat = np.arange(0, 100).reshape(10, 10)
mat[0, 1]
mat[4, 3]
mat[:, 0]
mat[5, :]
mat[:3, :3]
mat.shape
len(mat)   # <- attention
mat.size
mat.transpose()
```

Difference between lists and arrays?

```
# Masking!
array / 3
# my_list / 3   # This will raise an error since lists do not support element-wise division

array > 80
```

```
my_filter = array > 80
array[my_filter]
array[array > 50]

mat > 50
my_filter = mat > 50
mat[my_filter]
mat[mat > 50]

new_mat = np.array([[1, 2], [3, 4], [5, 6]])
```

EXCEPTIONS

Exceptions refer to events triggered by various types of errors.

Errors can be classified into categories such as:

- Syntactic
- Semantic
- Logical

Exceptions themselves can be categorized as:

- Managed
- Unmanaged

EXCEPTION HANDLING

```
- try
- except
- raise
```

```
...
1 / 0
a = 1
b = 0
print("Program start")
print("Division:", a/b)
print("Sum:", a+b)
print("End of program")

a = 1
b = 0
print("Program start")
try:
    print("Division:", a/b)
except ZeroDivisionError:
    print("Division by zero!")
print("Sum:", a+b)
print("End of program")
```

```
try:
    d = dict(arg)
except TypeError:
    print("The parameter cannot be converted to dict")
except NameError:
    print("The parameter does not exist")
except:
    print("Generic error")
raise ValueError("Error")

37 + "abc"
```

'else' and 'finally' clauses

```
numerator = 10
denominator = 0
try:
    quotient = numerator / denominator
except ZeroDivisionError:
    print("The denominator is null")
else:
    print("Quotient equals", quotient)
finally:
    print("End of program")
```

Function 'exc_info'

```
'''
It serves to know what kind of exception has occurred
'''
from sys import exc_info
numerator = 10
denominator = 0
try:
    quotient = numerator / denominator
except Exception:
```

```
    print("Error")
    print(exc_info())
else:
    print("Quotient equals", quotient)
finally:
    print("End of program")

...
```

Examples of exceptions:

```
- TypeError
- ValueError
- AttributeError
- IOError
- IndexError
- KeyboardInterrupt
- NameError
- StopIteration
- ZeroDivisionError
- ...
...
```

FUNCTIONS

CHAPTER 4

Python Functions

Functions in Python can be categorized into built-in, bookshelves, and user-defined. They are essentially snippets of code designed to execute operations on variables or objects. For every given input to a function, there exists a corresponding output.

Some examples of built-in functions include **dir()**, **help()**, **type()**, **print()**, and those from imported modules like **math**.

- **help() Function**: This function provides assistance by displaying information about a specified function, object, or library. For instance, **help(math)** would give details about the **math** module.
- **type() Function**: When provided with an object as an argument, this function reveals the data type of that object.
- **dir() Function**: It offers a glimpse into the attributes and methods associated with a given object. For example,

dir(math) would list the attributes and methods of the **math** module.

For custom functions, three primary components are essential:

1. **Name**: This identifies the function.
2. **Parameters**: These are the inputs that the function can process.
3. **Body**: This contains the actual code to execute within the function.

Here's an example of a custom function to calculate the cube of a number:

```
def cube_number(n):
    '''
    This function computes the cube of a given number.
    '''
    return n ** 3
```

Another example multiplies two given numbers:

```
def multiply_two_numbers(x, y):
    '''
    This function computes the product of two input values.
    '''
    return x * y
```

Multiple Return Values:

Functions can also return multiple values simultaneously. For instance:

```
def seas_and_mountains():
    return "seas", "mountains"

a, b = seas_and_mountains()
print(a, b)
```

Parameter Passing:

When calling functions, parameters can be passed in different ways. They can be positional or keyword-based:

```
def divide(numerator, denominator):
    return numerator / denominator
```

 # Different ways to call the function:

```
divide(155, 72)
divide(500, 20)
divide(numerator=500, denominator=20)
```

Default Values:

Functions can have default parameter values, which are used when no argument is provided during the function call:

```
def buy(item="eggs", quantity=10):
    print("Go buy", quantity, item)

buy()
buy(item="cheese")
```

 # In Jupyter:

Pressing **tab** after a function name displays possible parame-

ters, while **shift + tab** shows the function definition.
   Exercise:

```
def minimum_between_two_numbers(a, b, c):
    '''
    This function determines the minimum among three
    numbers and returns it.
    '''
    return min(a, b, c)
```

Example
Alternate Discount Function

```
def calculate_discount(amount, percentage=20):
    return amount * ((100 - percentage) / 100)

calculate_discount(amount=100)
calculate_discount(amount=100, percentage=17)
```

Applying Discount to a List of Prices

```
items_prices = [10, 40, 50, 60, 70, 100]
discounted_items_prices = [calculate_discount(amount)
for amount in items_prices]
print(discounted_items_prices)
```

Sample Dictionary and Discounting

```
products = {"t-shirt": 50, "hat": 70, "gloves": 100}
print(products)

print(products["hat"])
discounted_products = {item:
calculate_discount(amount, percentage=40) for item,
```

```
amount in products.items()}
print(discounted_products)
```

Built-in Functions Overview

```
print(dir(__builtins__))
help(abs)
abs_value = abs(-4)
```

Predefined Mathematical and Boolean Functions

```
'''
Predefined mathematical functions:
- min
- max
- sum
- pow
- abs
'''


'''
```

Default Boolean functions:

```
- all
Returns 'True' if all input parameters are true.
- any
Returns 'True' if some of the input parameters are
true.
```

```
'''
print(all([True, True, False]))
print(any([True, True, False]))
numbers = (5, 15, 25)
print(all([num > 10 for num in numbers]))
print(any([num > 10 for num in numbers]))

'''
```

Functions for iterations:

```
- map
- zip
- filter
'''
for item in zip([1, 2, 3, 4, 5], ["a", "b", "c", "d", "e"]):
    print(item)

for char in zip(range(6), "hello"):
    print(char)

def calculate_sum(x, y, z):
    return x + y + z

for total in map(calculate_sum, [1, 2], [5, 6], [10, 20]):
    print(total)

print(list(map(calculate_discount, items_prices)))

discount_values = [10, 20, 30, 40, 50]
print(list(map(calculate_discount, items_prices, discount_values)))

def is_greater_than_50(value):
```

```
    return value > 50

numbers_list = [10, 20, 30, 35, 70, 80, 110, 5, 3, 2]
for num in filter(is_greater_than_50, numbers_list):
    print(num)
```

SORTING FUNCTIONS:

- **sorted**

```
sorted(values)
```

- **The 'lambda' Operator** The **lambda** operator simplifies the writing of simple functions in one line.

```
def square(x):
    return x**2

square(5)

square2 = lambda x: x**2
list(map(square2, values))
list(map(lambda x: x**2, values))

for n in filter(lambda x: x > 50, values):
    print(n)
```

THE CLASSES

Define a class

```
class Food:
    pass
```

Instance of a class -> object

```
pasta = Food()
```

Methods

```
class Food:
    '''
    A class example for managing the nutritional
    values of foods.
    '''
```

```
    def __init__(self, prot, carb, gras):
        self.protein = prot
        self.carbohydrates = carb
        self.fats = gras
        '''
        - The '__init__' method is the constructor of
        the class.
        - The first parameter of the constructor is
        always 'self', but we don't have to
          specify it when we create an instance.
        '''
```

Example instances

```
pasta = Food(prot=13, carb=74, gras=1)
print(pasta.carbohydrates)

pizza = Food(prot=10, carb=30, gras=12)
print(pizza.fats)  # Corrected 'fat' to 'fats'
print(pizza.protein)

strange = Food(prot="abc", carb=-72, gras=[5, 6])  #
<- Does it work?
```

We add controls to the constructor on the input data

```
class Food:
    '''
    A class example for managing the nutritional
    values of foods.
    '''

    def __init__(self, prot, carb, gras):
        # CHECK: Is the data all numeric?
        if not all([type(elem) in (int, float) for
```

```
        elem in (prot, carb, gras)]):
            raise Exception("Enter only whole numbers
            or numbers with commas.")

        # CHECK: Is the data all positive?
        elif any([prot < 0, carb < 0, gras < 0]):
            raise Exception("Nutrient values cannot
            be negative.")

        # If everything is okay, create the instance!
        else:
            self.protein = prot
            self.carbohydrates = carb
            self.fats = gras
```

Example instances with error cases

```
diet_coke = Food(prot=5, carb=5, gras=-100)   # <-
Error
alien_food = Food(prot=6, carb="space", gras=9)   # <-
Error
```

ADDING A METHOD TO THE CLASS

```
class Food:
    '''
    An illustration of a class handling nutritional
    values of foods.
    '''
    def __init__(self, prot, carb, gras):
        # VALIDATION: Are all data entries numeric?
        if not all(isinstance(elem, (int, float)) for
        elem in (prot, carb, gras)):
```

```
            raise Exception("Please input only whole
            numbers or numbers with decimals.")
```

VALIDATION: Are all data entries positive?

```
elif any(prot < 0, carb < 0, gras < 0):
            raise Exception("Nutritional values
            should not be negative.")

        # If validations pass, instantiate the object!
        else:
            self.protein = prot
            self.carbohydrates = carb
            self.fats = gras

    def calculate_calories(self):
        return self.protein * 4 + self.carbohydrates
        * 4 + self.fats * 9
```

Example usage:

```
pasta = Food(prot=13, carb=74, gras=1)
print(pasta.calculate_calories())

pizza = Food(prot=10, carb=30, gras=12)
print(pizza.calculate_calories())
```

Alternatively, you can define and add a method separately:

```
def calculate_calories(self):
    return self.protein * 4 + self.carbohydrates * 4
    + self.fats * 9
```

Add the method to the class using:

```
Food.calculate_calories = calculate_calories

'''
- A method is essentially a function associated with
an object.
- An attribute represents the data that defines it.
- The concept of "encapsulation" is central.
---> This is the foundation of 'object-oriented
programming'.
'''
```

Another example:

```
class Cat:
    def __init__(self, name, color, age, race):
        self.name = name
        self.color = color
        self.age = age
        self.race = race

cat1 = Cat("Sylvester", "Black", 3, "Soriano")
print(cat1.name)
print(cat1.color)
print(cat1.race)
```

CLASS METHODS

```
class Cat:
    def __init__(self, name, color, age, race):
        self.name = name
        self.color = color
```

```
        self.age = age
        self.race = race

    def towards(self):
        print("meow")

    def purr(self):
        print("purr")

cat2 = Cat("Gibson", "Pezzato", 6, "Balinese")
cat2.towards()
cat2.purr()
```

Inheritance

```
'''
- Define a class based on a pre-existing class, which
then "inherits" its
methods and attributes.
- The "upper" class generalizes, while the "lower"
class specifies.
'''

class Vegetable(Food):
    def __init__(self, prot, carb):
        self.fat = 0
        self.protein = prot
        self.carbohydrates = carb
```

Create an instance

```
eggplant = Vegetable(prot=1.5, carb=2.5)
print(eggplant.calculate_calories())
```

Another version, more correct

```
'''
In this way, we don't lose all the controls and logic
already implemented.
'''

class Vegetable(Food):
    def __init__(self, prot, carb):
        super().__init__(prot=prot, carb=carb, fat=0)
        # We add specific features

class Vegetable(Food):
    def __init__(self, prot, carb, etic):
        # Call the constructor of the previous class
        # to manage the data of the 'Food' class
        super().__init__(prot=prot, carb=carb, fat=0)
```

Let's manage the specific data of the 'Vegetable' class

```
    if not isinstance(etic, str):
            raise Exception("The label must be a
            string.")
        else:
            self.label = etic

    def evaluate_label(self):
        if self.label == "certified":
            print("Great label")
        else:
            print("Mediocre label")

carrot = Vegetable(prot=1, carb=7, etic="certified")
print(carrot.carbohydrates)
print(carrot.calculate_calories())
carrot.evaluate_label()
```

PROPERTIES

```
'''
- Use a class method as if it were an attribute
'''
Food.calories = property(calculate_calories)
eggplants.calories
pasta.calories
```

Properties defining attributes

```
class Vegetable(Food):
    def __init__(self, protein=0, carbohydrates=0):
        self.fat = 0
        self.protein = protein
        self.carbohydrates = carbohydrates

    def get_carbohydrates(self):
        return self.carbohydrates

    def set_carbohydrates(self,
    new_value_carbohydrates):
        self.carbohydrates = new_value_carbohydrates

    carbohydrates = property(get_carbohydrates,
    set_carbohydrates)

    def get_protein(self):
        return self.protein

    def set_protein(self, new_value_protein):
        self.protein = new_value_protein

    protein = property(get_protein, set_protein)
```

```
    def get_fat(self):
        return self.fat

    def set_fat(self, new_fat_value):
        if new_fat_value > 0:
            raise Exception("Vegetables have no fat")
        self.fat = new_fat_value

    fat = property(get_fat, set_fat)
carrot = Vegetable(1, 7)
carrot.calories
carrot.carbohydrates
carrot.carbohydrates = 20
carrot.fat
carrot.fat = 5
```

Private methods

```
'''
- Methods that cannot be called from outside the
class they belong to
- By naming convention, they begin with '__' (e.g.,
'__init__')
'''
class Archive:
    def __open_file__(self):
        print("a private method")
```

Special Methods

```
'''
- Allow you to adapt the "classic" Python methods to
new classes
- For example: 'len', 'str'
'''
```

Redefine the method '__len__'

```
class Video:
    def __init__(self, name, duration):
        self.name = name
        self.duration = duration

    def __len__(self):
        return self.duration

vlog1 = Video(name="I talk about me", duration=12)
print(len(vlog1))

list_example = [1, 2, 3]
dir(list_example)   # Contains special (and private)
methods

dir(vlog1)   # Special methods are already present!
print(vlog1)
str(vlog1)   # They have default functions
```

Redefine the '__str__' method

```
class Video:
    def __init__(self, name, duration):
        self.name = name
        self.duration = duration

    def __len__(self):
        return self.duration

    def __str__(self):
        return "Video titled '{0}'".format(self.name)

vlog2 = Video(name="I show you my room", duration=5)
```

```
print(str(vlog1))
print(str(vlog2))
```

INPUT AND OUTPUT

Function 'print'

```
help(print)
for n in range(3):
    print("The value of 'n' is:", n)

for n in range(3):
    print("The value of 'n' is:", n, sep="")

for n in range(3):
    print("The value of 'n' is:", n, sep="", end=", ")
```

FILE

CHAPTER 4

```python
'''
- Python provides the 'open' function for file
operations.
'''
myfile = open("test.txt", "w")

'''
- With the previous instruction, a file named
'test.txt' (in the working directory) will be created
or overwritten.
'''
'''
Parameters:
- 'w': write
- 'r': read
- 'a': append
'''
dir(myfile)
myfile.name
myfile.mode
myfile.closed
myfile.write("I write in the file.")
myfile.close()
myfile.closed

myfile = open("test.txt", "r")
myfile.readline()
myfile.close()

other_file = open("other_test.txt", "w")
other_file.write("Various things.\n")
other_file.write("Other stuff.\n")
other_file.write("And text.")
other_file.close()

other_file = open("other_test.txt", "r")
```

```
for line in other_file.readlines():
    print(line.strip())
other_file.close()
```

Exercise on Spyder

```
print("Enter numbers")
my_list = []
for n in range(5):
    num = input()
    my_list.append(num)

the_file = open("my_list.txt", "w")
for element in my_list:
    the_file.write(element)
    the_file.write("\n")
the_file.close()

print("File has been written.")
```

5

Chapter 5

FINDING ERRORS

Avoid searching for errors merely by adding or removing print statements. Instead, utilize a debugging tool! If you're not accustomed to using debugging tools regularly, you're causing yourself undue frustration and wasting time.

Python's Native Debugger, PDB

Although Python's built-in debugger, PDB, may seem basic, understanding its functionality is crucial for two main reasons:

1. PDB serves as a foundation for more advanced debugging tools. Familiarizing yourself with PDB can enhance your proficiency with these tools.
2. I'll demonstrate how to optimize PDB's utility as a standalone debugger.

Here's a breakdown of PDB's evolving utility:

- The fundamental version.
- Basic version enhanced with smart use of macros.
- The basic version integrated with the Emacs text editor.
- The basic version coupled with the DDD graphical interface for debugging.

Core Components

You can find PDB within the 'lib' subfolder of your Python installation. For example, on a Unix system, it might be located in directories like **/usr/lib/python2.2** or **/usr/local/lib/python2.4**. To debug an **x.py** script, input:

```
% /usr/lib/python2.2/pdb.py x.py
```

(Include command-line arguments after 'x.py' if necessary).

Given the frequent use of PDB, it's advisable to set up an alias. In Unix's C shell, you could set it as:

```
alias pdb=/usr/lib/python2.2/pdb.py
```

This allows for a simpler command:

```
% pdb x.py
```

Within PDB, set your initial breakpoint, e.g., at line 12:

```
b 12
```

You can make this conditional, like:

```
b 12, z > 5
```

Type 'c' to continue, which will execute **x.py** and halt at the breakpoint. Then, proceed with main operations, similar to those in GDB:

- 'b' to set a breakpoint
- 'tbreak' for a one-time breakpoint
- 'ignore' to skip a breakpoint k times (where k is specified)
- 'l' to display source code lines
- 'n' to move to the next line, bypassing function code
- 's' to step into a function when called
- 'c' to proceed to the next breakpoint
- 'w' for a stack report

- 'u' to ascend a stack level, e.g., to inspect local variables
- 'd' to descend a stack level
- 'r' to resume until the active function returns
- 'j' to skip to a specific line without executing intermediary code
- 'h' for concise online help (e.g., 'h b' for help on 'b'; 'h' for a command list; 'h pdb' for a PDB tutorial)
- 'q' to exit PDB

Initiating PDB will present its prompt, 'Pdb'. With multifile programs, specify breakpoints as 'module name:line number'. For instance, with the main module **x.py** and an imported **y.py**, set a breakpoint on line 8 of **y.py**:

```
(Pdb) b y:8
```

Remember, this is only possible after importing **y** from **x**.

When using PDB, you're essentially in Python's interactive mode. Thus, you can input any Python command. Although PDB has a 'p' command for variable and expression values, it's often redundant. Typing a variable's name in interactive Python will print its value, just as 'p' would. Instead of:

```
(Pdb) p ww
```

Simply type:

```
ww
```

The value of 'ww' will be displayed.

For intricate data structures, create a function to display them. Then, call this function within PDB for more nuanced, context-specific printing.

After your program encounters PDB or a runtime error, restart without exiting PDB to retain breakpoints by entering 'c'. If you've modified your source code, these changes will be updated in PDB.

For commands like 'n' in Python lines with multiple operations, use them repeatedly or set a temporary breakpoint to override. For example, for the operation:

```
for i in range(10):
```

You'd need to use 'n' twice. Similarly, for:

```
y = [(y,x) for (x,y) in x]
```

With **x** having 10 elements, use 'n' 10 times. Setting a breakpoint can prevent this repetitive action.

USING PDB MACROS

The inherently sparse nature of PDB can be somewhat alleviated by effectively utilizing the alias command, which I strongly recommend. For instance, type:

```
alias c c;; l
```

This configuration ensures that each time you continue execution and reach a breakpoint, you will automatically receive a listing of the surrounding code. This feature significantly compensates for the lack of a graphical user interface (GUI) in PDB.

Given its importance, it's advisable to incorporate this alias into your PDB initialization file. In Unix systems, this file is typically located at **$HOME/.pdbrc35**. By doing so, the alias remains consistently available. Similarly, you can enhance the n and s commands with the following aliases:

```
alias n n;;; l
alias s s;;l
```

PDB also offers an **unalias** command to remove an existing alias.

You can also create other macros tailored to specific programs you are debugging. For instance, if you have a variable named **ww** in **x.py** and wish to inspect its value whenever the debugger pauses at breakpoints, modify the earlier alias as follows:

```
alias c c;; l;; ww
```

Using __dict__

We will demonstrate that if **o** is an object of a certain class, printing **o.__dict__** will display all the member variables associated with that object. This capability can be combined with PDB's alias features, such as:

```
alias c c;; l;;o.__dict__
```

However, for a more generic approach, consider using:

```
alias c c;; l;;self
```

This configuration provides information about member variables irrespective of the class context. Nonetheless, this method may not reveal information about member variables in the parent class.

The type() function

When examining someone else's code, or even your own, determining the type of object a variable represents can sometimes be unclear. In such cases, the **type()** function proves to be invaluable.

Here are some illustrative examples:

```
>>> x = [5,12,13]
>>> type(x)
<type 'list'>
>>> type(3)
<type 'int'>
>>> def f(y): return y*y
...
>>> f(5)
25
>>> type(f)
<type 'function'>
```

Using PDB with Emacs

Emacs serves as both a text editor and a toolkit for various tasks. Many software developers highly recommend its capabilities. It is available on Windows, Mac, and Unix/Linux systems, with most Linux distributions including it by default. Even if you're not a die-hard Emacs fan, it can still be an effective tool for utilizing PDB. You can split Emacs into dual windows: one for programming and the other for PDB. This allows you to track your code's progress in real-time while navigating through it.

To begin, let's consider a Python file named x.py. Open your terminal or command prompt based on your operating system and enter either:

```
emacs x.py
```

or

```
emacs -nw x.py
```

The former launches Emacs in a new window with graphical interface features, whereas the latter starts Emacs within the current window, supporting text-only operations. We'll refer to the former as "GUI mode". Next, input **M-x pdb**. Note that "M" typically represents the Escape (or Alt) key rather than the literal letter 'M'. You'll be prompted to specify how to initiate PDB. Provide the same command you'd use to run PDB externally to Emacs but with the complete path, for instance:

```
/usr/local/lib/python2.4/pdb.py x.py 3 8
```

Here, the numbers 3 and 8 represent command-line arguments for your program.

Subsequently, Emacs will bifurcate into two windows as mentioned earlier. You can establish breakpoints within the PDB window or by pressing **C-x space** at the desired line in the programming window, where "C" signifies holding down the Control key while pressing the subsequent key. Then, initiate PDB as you usually would.

If you make alterations to your program using the GUI Emacs mode, press **IMPython | Rescan** to update PDB with the latest version of your code.

Another benefit of using Emacs in this scenario is its Python mode, offering specialized Python editing commands, which will be elaborated upon later.

Regarding basic editing commands, you can search for "Emacs tutorials" or "Emacs commands" online for a plethora of resources. Here, we'll offer just enough information to kickstart your journey.

Firstly, understand the concept of buffers in Emacs. Each file you edit has its dedicated buffer. Any action you perform also generates a corresponding buffer. For instance, invoking Emacs' online help commands creates a buffer, which you can edit or save if needed. An example pertinent to PDB is when you execute **M-x pdb**, resulting in a new buffer. At times, you might have multiple buffers or even multiple windows, but for simplicity, we'll focus on having two.

Below, we present commands suitable for both Emacs versions: the text-only variant and the GUI version. Nevertheless, text commands are usable in the GUI mode as well.

CHAPTER 5

action	text	GUI
slider movement	Direction keys, Page Up/Down	mouse, left scrollbar
cancel	C-x u	Edit | Undo
cut	C-space (cursor move) C-w	select region | Edit | Cut
paste	C-y	Edit | Paste
string search	C-s	Edit | Search

select region	C-@	select region
go to other window	C-x or	click window
enlarge window	(1 line at a time) C-x ^	drag bar
repeat the following commands n times	M-x n	M-x n
list bufer	C-x C-b	Bufers
go to a bufer	C-x b	Bufers
exit Emacs	C-x C-c	File | Exit Emacs

When working with PDBs, remember that your PDB buffer's name should begin with "gud", like gudx.py. To view a list of Python's unique functions in Emacs, use the shortcut Ch d and search in python mode (pythonmode). A distinctive feature of Emacs' python mode is its automatic self-indentation; it will add extra indentation after lines containing def or class.

Below are some operations:

action	text	GUI
comment region	C-space (move cursors) C-c #	select region | Python | Comment
go to the beginning of def or class	ESC C-a	ESC C-a
go to the end of def or class	ESC C-e	ESC C-e
go into external block	C-c C-u	C-c C-u
move region to the right	mark region,C-c C-r	mark region, Python | Shift right
move region to the left	mark region,C-c C-l	mark region, Python | Shift left

www.ingramcontent.com/pod-product-compliance
Lightning Source LLC
LaVergne TN
LVHW021048100526
838202LV00079B/5063